D1487107

DRAW
CARTOON
PEOPLE
in 4 Easy Steps

Then Write a Story

1

2

3

4

Stephanie LaBaff
Illustrated by Tom LaBaff

Enslow Elementary
an imprint of

Enslow Publishers, Inc.
40 Industrial Road
Box 398
Berkeley Heights, NJ 07922
USA

http://www.enslow.com

Enslow Elementary, an imprint of Enslow Publishers, Inc.

Enslow Elementary® is a registered trademark of Enslow Publishers, Inc.

Library of Congress Cataloging-in-Publication Data
LaBaff, Stephanie.
  Draw cartoon people in 4 easy steps : then write a story / Stephanie LaBaff.
      p. cm. — (Drawing in 4 easy steps)
  Includes index.
  Summary: "Learn to draw people, objects, and faces and how to write a story about them, with a story example and story prompts"—Provided by publisher.
  ISBN 978-0-7660-3843-1
  1. Human beings—Caricatures and cartoons—Juvenile literature. 2. Cartooning—Technique—Juvenile literature. 3. Drawing—Technique—Juvenile literature. 4. Comic books, strips, etc.—Authorship—Juvenile literature. I. Title. II. Title: Draw cartoon people in four easy steps.
  NC1764.8.H84L33 2012
  741.5'1—dc23
                                        2011018040
Paperback ISBN 978-1-4644-0016-2
ePUB ISBN 978-1-4645-0461-7
PDF ISBN 978-1-4646-0461-4

Printed in the United States of America
092011 Lake Book Manufacturing, Inc., Melrose Park, IL

10 9 8 7 6 5 4 3 2 1

Illustration Credits: Tom LaBaff

To Our Readers: We have done our best to make sure all Internet Addresses in this book were active and appropriate when we went to press. However, the author and the publisher have no control over and assume no liability for the material available on those Internet sites or on other Web sites they may link to. Any comments or suggestions can be sent by e-mail to comments@enslow.com or to the address on the back cover.

♻ Enslow Publishers, Inc., is committed to printing our books on recycled paper. The paper in every book contains 10% to 30% post-consumer waste (PCW). The cover board on the outside of each book contains 100% PCW. Our goal is to do our part to help young people and the environment too!

Contents

Getting Started

Lots of Paper

Pencil sharpener

your imagination

↑ Pencil

Eraser

ARTIST'S SURVIVAL KIT

Drawing cartoon people is as easy as 1, 2, 3, 4! Follow the 4 steps for each picture in this book. You will be amazed at what you can draw. After some practice, you will be able to make your own adjustments, too. Change a pose, move a leg, or draw a different face. There are lots of possibilities!

Follow the 4 Steps

1 Start with big shapes, such as the body.

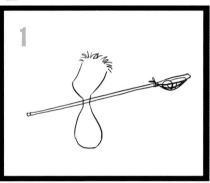

2 Add smaller shapes, such as the arms and legs. In each step, new lines are shown in red.

3 Continue adding new lines. Erase lines as needed.

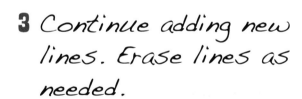

4 Add final details and color. Your cartoon will come to life!

Chip

1

2

3

4

Coach

1

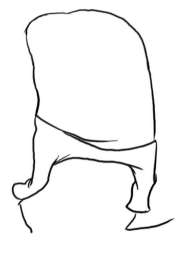

2

Erase the dotted lines at the shoulders and arms.

3

4

Policeman

1

2

Erase the dotted line under the arm.

3 Erase the dotted line behind the hat.

4

Superfan

1

2

Erase the dotted line at the right arm.

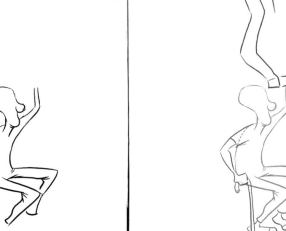

3

Erase the dotted line at the left arm.

4

Fred

1

2

Cartoon tough guys usually have a huge upper body and skinny legs.

Erase the dotted li[ne] behind the head.

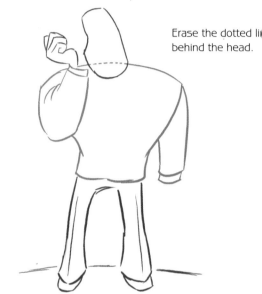

3

4

Cheesehead

1

2

3

4

Frannie

1

Put a shadow under her foot to show she's tiptoeing.

2

Erase the dotted line behind the legs.

3

4

Harry

1

2

Erase the dotted line at the shoulder.

3

Erase the dotted line behind the box, right arm, and left hand.

4

Joey

1

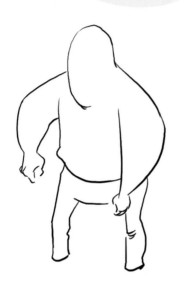

2

Erase the dotted line behind his right sleeve.

3

Erase the dotted line behind the broom and the dustpan.

4

14

Peanut

1

2

Erase the dotted line behind the nose and his left shoulder.

3

Erase the dotted line at his hands, belly, left arm, and right foot.

4

Terry

1

2

Erase the dotted line at the right arm and leg.

3

4

Ticket Taker

1

2

Erase the dotted line at the neck, shoulder, hand, and leg.

3

Erase the dotted line at her left sleeve.

4

Tickets

Waterboy

1

2

Erase the dotted line at the nec[k,] shoulder, hand, and foot.

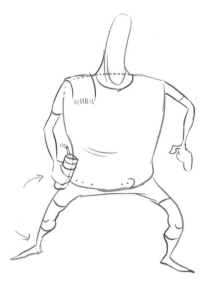

3

4

Duke

1

2

Erase the dotted line at the shoulders.

3

4

Mascot

1

2

Erase the dotted line behind the beak and right arm.

3

4

Archer Amy

1

2

Erase the dotted line at the shoulders and leg.

3

Erase the dotted line at the hands and fingers.

4

Duncan

1

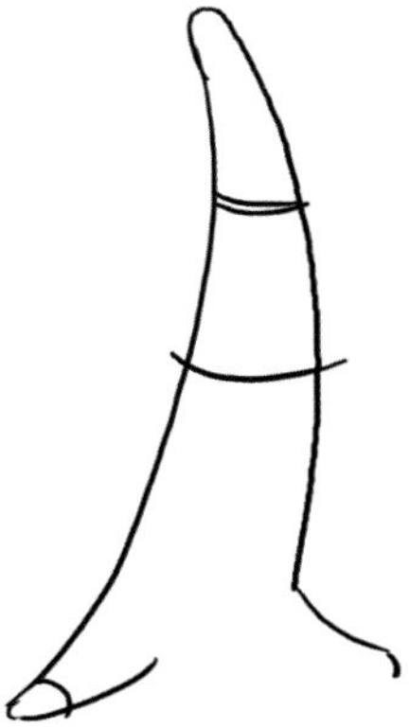

2

Erase the dotted lin
at the shoulders
and hand.

3

Erase the line
behind the hairline.

4

Mega Meg

1

2

Erase the dotted line at the shoulders and legs.

3

4

Fishhook Frank

1

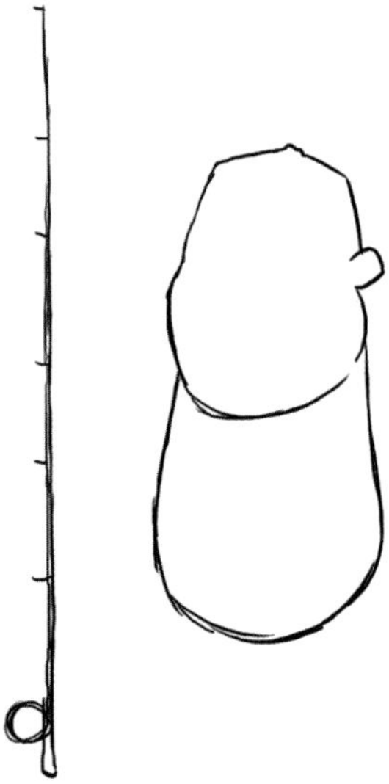

2

3

Erase the dotted line at the brim of the hat.

4

Lax Larry

1

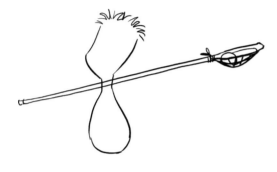

2

Erase the dotted line at the hands, neck, and legs.

3

Erase the dotted line at the nose.

4

Ninja

1

2

3

Erase the dotted line at the shoulder.

4

Conehead

1

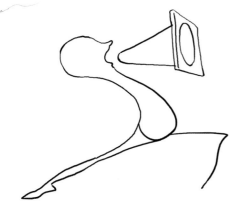

2

Erase the dotted line at the hand, shoulders, and legs.

3

Erase the dotted line at the leg.

4

Football

1

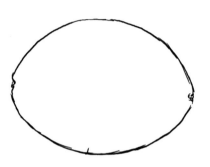

2

3

4

Popcorn

1

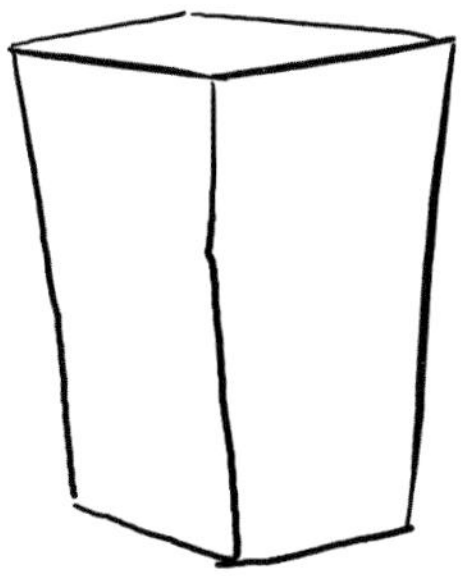

2

Erase the dotted line behind the triangles.

3

4

Secret ops hi-tech security cameras.

Trophy

1

2

3

Erase the dotted line at the right leg.

4

Worried

1

2

3

Worried expressions are all about making wide eyes and biting lips!

Sink the head into her shoulders.

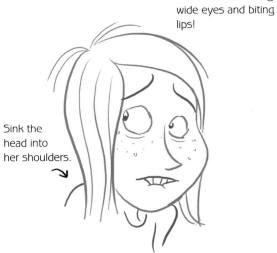

4

Laughing

1

2

Throw his head back to make it look like he must have heard a very funny joke.

3

Add action lines.

4

Sleepy

1

Droopy ears help show what he's feeling.

2

3

4

Sagging head and hair help make gravity look like his enemy!

Thrilled

1

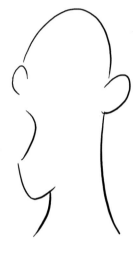

2

Erase the dotted line at the upper lip.

3

Don't be afraid to stretch out his expression. It's just a cartoon!

4

Angry

1

2

Erase the dotted lines under the hair.

3

4

How to Write a Story

Write a Story in 5 Easy Steps

Are you ready to write a story to go with your drawings? Maybe you have a story you want to illustrate. Follow these five simple steps to make your very own story with drawings.

Step 1: Prewriting

Do you want to write about people? Maybe you have an idea for a story about people at a football game. Keep in mind the drawings you want to use and base your story around them.

One way to begin your story is to
answer these questions: Who? What?
Why? Where? When? How?
For example:
Who is the main character?
What happens to him in your story?
Why is the story interesting?
Where and when does he live?
How does he earn money?

Here is a good brainstorming exercise. Fold a paper into six columns. Write the words *Who? What? Why? Where? When?* and *How?* at the top of each column. Write down every answer that comes into your head in the matching column. Do this for about five or ten minutes. Take a look at your list and pick out the ideas that you like the best. Now you are ready to write your story.

Cartoon Story Starters

Archer Amy had her arrow notched and and ready to go . . .

The policeman saw the robbers as they ran down the dark alley . . .

Ninja came to the ladies' rescue just seconds before . . .

Superfan was there for every game until one Saturday when . . .

The team mascot was missing. What could have happened to him? . . .

Just when they were about to call the game, Mega Meg yelled . . .

Step 2: *Writing*

Use the ideas from the list you made in Step 1. Write your story all the way through. Don't stop to make changes. You can always make changes later.

A story about cartoon people who sit and watch TV is not very interesting. What could happen to the people? What if they went to a football game? Your story will be more exciting if you don't make things too easy for your characters.

Step 3: Editing

Read your story. Is there a way to make it better? Rewrite the parts that you can improve. You might want to ask a friend or teacher to help. Ask them for their ideas.

Step 4: Proofreading

Make sure the spelling, punctuation, and grammar are correct.

Storyboarding

It's time to see how your story works with your drawings. Find a table or other flat surface. Spread your drawings out in the order that goes with your story. Then place the matching text below each drawing. When you have your story the way you like it, go to Step 5. You can pick a way to publish your story.

Step 5: *Publishing Your Book*

You can make your story into a book. There are many different forms your book can take. Here are a few ideas:

⭐ Simple book – Staple sheets of blank paper together along their edges.

⭐ Folded book – Fold sheets of blank paper in half, then staple on the fold.

⭐ Hardcover book – Buy a blank hardcover book. Then write your finished story in the book, leaving spaces to add your art.

⭐ Bound book – Punch a few holes along the edges of some pieces of paper. Tie them up or fill the holes with paper fasteners. There are many fun and colorful binding options at office supply stores.

★ Digital book – Create a digital book using your computer. There are some great programs available. Ask an adult to help you find one that is right for you.

Our Story

You have finished the five steps of writing and illustrating a story. We bet you created a great story! Want to see ours? Turn the page and take a peek.

Trophy Trouble

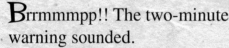

Brrmmmpp!! The two-minute warning sounded.

"That's our cue!" whispered Chip to his partner, Birdman, as they hid near the locker room. "You know what to do!"

Birdman ran to the guard at the locker room door. He snatched the guard's hat off his head and ran down the hall, cawing and flapping his wings. The furious guard chased after him.

As soon as they were gone, Chip made his move. He slipped into the locker room and snatched the Heisman Trophy from its case. "Mission accomplished!" he

thought. But as he turned to make his getaway, he saw that he was not alone. Perched in a corner was Archer Amy, and her arrow was pointed at him! Before he could move, she let the arrow fly, pinning Chip's shirt to the wall. She leaped over and grabbed the trophy.

"It's a good thing I overheard your talk with Birdman," she said. "I'll make sure this gets back to its owner." But as Amy headed for the door, in rushed Waterboy. He tackled her to the ground. Amy knew she didn't stand a chance against the 300-pound Waterboy,

so she hit the silent alarm button on her watch. Within moments, a shadow moved along the wall. Amy glanced up and saw her friend, Ninja. Amy tossed the trophy to her while continuing to wrestle Waterboy. Ninja caught the trophy and placed it safely aside. Then she pounced on Waterboy and touched his neck, causing him to collapse into a deep sleep.

"Thanks for coming so fast!" said Amy as she stood and wiped herself off. Just then, two men rushed into the room. One wore a dark suit and sunglasses; the other was dressed as a peanut.

"Oh no, not more of them!" Amy cried.

"Don't worry, we're on your side!" said the man in the suit. "I'm Fred, FBI agent, and this peanut man is an undercover agent. We've been after these thieves for months. They've been stealing valuable sports memorabilia." He looked at Chip pinned to the wall and Waterboy on the floor. "It looks like you've done our job for us. Thank you!"

Amy smiled and pointed to the trophy, now back in its case. "No problem. But from now on, you might want to put a better lock on that thing."

Further Reading

Books

Artell, Mike. *Funny Cartooning for Kids.* New York: Sterling Publishing, 2006.

Bergin, Mark. *How to Draw Cartoons.* New York: Rosen Publishing, 2010.

Boynton, Sandra. *Amazing Cows: Udder Absurdity for Children.* New York: Workman Publishing, 2010.

Roche, Art. *Art for Kids: Cartooning.* New York: Sterling Publishing, 2010.

Silverstein, Shel. *Don't Bump the Gump! and Other Fantasies.* New York: HarperCollins, 2008.

Internet Addresses

Cartoon Network. 2011.
<http://www.cartoonnetwork.com>

Cartoon Stock. Kids Cartoons and Comics. 2012.
<http://www.cartoonstock.com/newscartoons/directory/k/kids.asp>

National Geographic Kids. Cartoons. 2011.
<http://kids.nationalgeographic.com/kids/activities/cartoons>

Index